W9-CQD-307

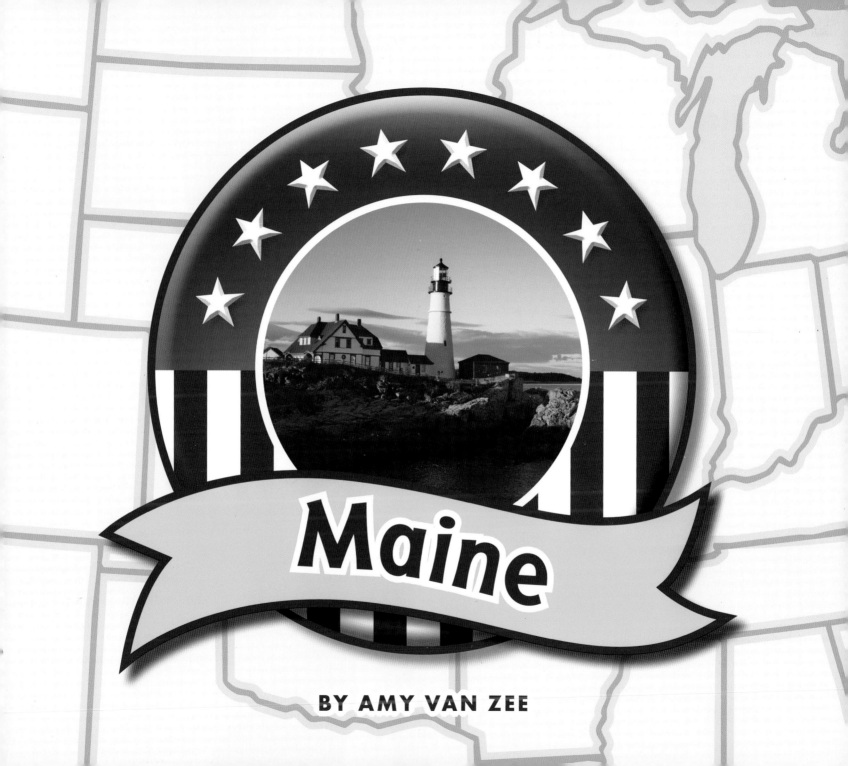

Maine

BY AMY VAN ZEE

The Child's World

Published by The Child's World®
1980 Lookout Drive • Mankato, MN 56003-1705
800-599-READ • www.childsworld.com

ACKNOWLEDGMENTS
The Child's World®: Mary Berendes, Publishing Director
The Design Lab: Design and production
Red Line Editorial: Editorial direction

PHOTO CREDITS: Doug Lemke/Shutterstock Images, cover, 1, 3; Matt Kania/
Map Hero, Inc., 4, 5; Denis Jr. Tangney/iStockphoto, 7; iStockphoto, 9, 10;
Greg Nicholas/iStockphoto, 11; james boulette/iStockphoto, 13; Photolibrary,
15; Stephen Muskie/iStockphoto, 17; Seth Wenig/AP Images, 19; One Mile
Up, 22; Quarter-dollar coin image from the United States Mint, 22

LIBRARY OF CONGRESS CATALOGING-IN-PUBLICATION DATA
Van Zee, Amy.
  Maine / by Amy Van Zee.
       p. cm.
Includes bibliographical references and index.
ISBN 978-1-60253-463-6 (library bound : alk. paper)
1. Maine—Juvenile literature. I. Title.

F19.3.V36 2010
974.1—dc22

                                    2010017715

Printed in the United States of America in Mankato, Minnesota.
July 2010
F11538

On the cover:
The Portland
Head Light is
about 70 feet
(21 m) tall.

CONTENTS

Geography

Let's explore Maine! Maine is in the northeast United States. This area is called New England. Maine shares a long border with Canada. The Atlantic Ocean is to the south.

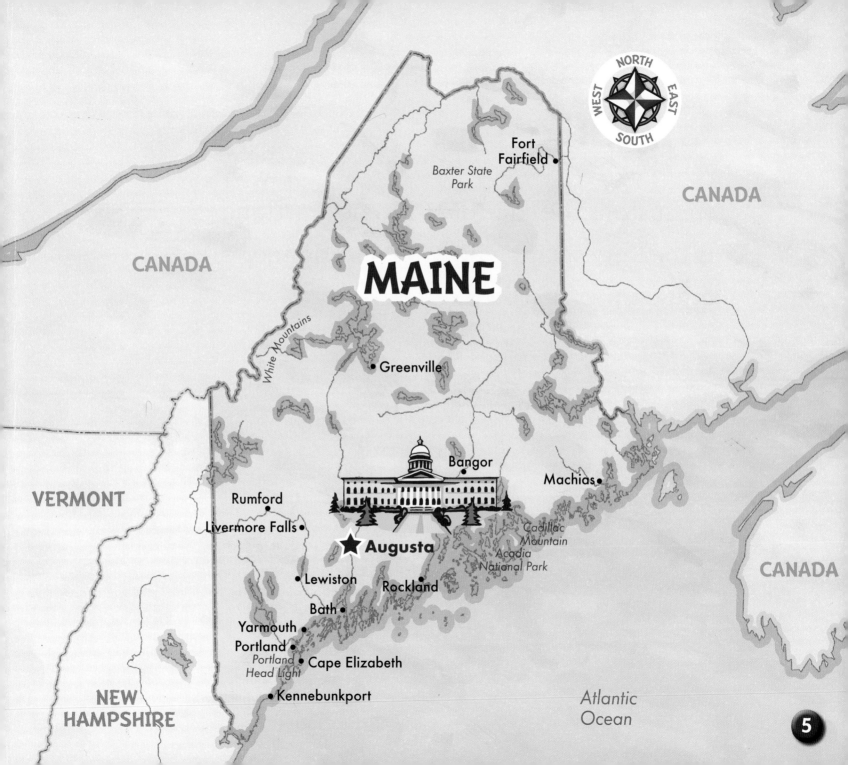

CANADA

CANADA

Fort
Fairfield

Baxter State
Park

MAINE

White Mountains

Greenville

Bangor

Machias

VERMONT

Rumford

Livermore Falls

★ Augusta

Cadillac
Mountain
Acadia
National Park

Lewiston

Rockland

CANADA

Bath

Yarmouth

Portland
Portland
Head Light

Cape Elizabeth

Kennebunkport

NEW
HAMPSHIRE

Atlantic
Ocean

NORTH
WEST   EAST
SOUTH

Cities

Augusta is the capital of Maine. Portland is the largest city. Lewiston and Bangor are other large cities in the state.

Portland is on the eastern coast of Maine. ▶

Land

The southern coast of Maine has many beaches. The White Mountains stretch across the northwest corner of the state. Maine also has many lakes, rivers, and streams.

Baxter State Park is a **popular** place for **hiking** and camping in Maine. ▶

Plants and Animals

Most of Maine is covered in forests. Many types of trees grow in the cool weather here. The state tree is the white pine. Maine's state bird is the chickadee. Its call sounds like a whistle. The state flower is the white pinecone and the needles from the white pine.

Many pine trees grow in the forests of Maine. ▶

Because it has so many pine trees, Maine is called "the Pine Tree State."

11

People and Work

More than 1.3 million people live in Maine. About half the people in Maine live in **urban** areas. Many people travel to Maine to see its forests, beaches, and mountains. Some people in Maine work in jobs that help these travelers. Others work in **manufacturing**, logging, and fishing.

This logging truck carried logs across Maine. ▶

History

Native Americans have lived in the Maine area for thousands of years. People from England and France came to the area in the 1600s and 1700s. In the 1600s, the Maine area became part of the Massachusetts Bay **Colony**. Maine became the twenty-third state on March 15, 1820.

Some of the first settlers in Maine were loggers in the White Mountains. ▶

Ways of Life

Many people in Maine enjoy outdoor activities. Fishing, swimming, and skiing are popular. The Maine Lobster **Festival** is held during the first weekend in August. Visitors can see **parades**, arts, and crafts.

More than 2,000 pounds (907 kg) of lobster have been cooked at the Maine Lobster Festival in one year!

A man fishes on the Maine coast on a foggy summer morning. ▶

Famous People

Writer Stephen King was born in Maine. Poet Henry Wadsworth Longfellow was born in the state in 1807. Former U.S. Vice President Nelson Aldrich Rockefeller was born in Maine, too.

Stephen King has written many books. ▶

Famous Places

The Portland Head Light is one of the oldest **lighthouses** in the United States. It was built in 1791. Acadia National Park in southern Maine has mountains, beaches, lakes, and forests.

Cadillac Mountain in Acadia National Park is the highest mountain on the Atlantic coast of the ▶ United States. It is 1,530 feet (466 m) tall.

State Symbols

Seal

Maine's state seal shows a farmer and a seaman. They stand for farming and fishing. Go to childsworld.com/links for a link to Maine's state Web site, where you can get a firsthand look at the state seal.

Flag

The state flag has the state seal on it. The moose and the pine tree on the seal stand for nature.

Quarter

A lighthouse is on the Maine state quarter. The quarter came out in 2003.

Glossary

colony (KOL-uh-nee): A colony is an area of land that is newly settled and is controlled by a government of another land. The Maine area was once a part of the Massachusetts Bay Colony.

festival (FESS-tih-vul): A festival is a celebration for an event or holiday. The Maine Lobster Festival is held each year.

hiking (HYK-ing): Hiking is taking a walk in a natural area, such as a hill or a mountain. Many people enjoy hiking in Maine.

lighthouses (LYT-howss-ez): Lighthouses are tall buildings near oceans or large lakes that use lights to warn ships of danger. Visitors to Maine can see lighthouses.

manufacturing (man-yuh-FAK-chur-ing): Manufacturing is the task of making items with machines. Some people in Maine work in manufacturing jobs.

parades (puh-RAYDZ): Parades are when people march to honor holidays. Visitors to the Maine Lobster Festival can see parades.

popular (POP-yuh-lur): To be popular is to be enjoyed by many people. Fishing and skiing are popular activities in Maine.

seal (SEEL): A seal is a symbol a state uses for government business. A farmer is on the Maine state seal.

symbols (SIM-bulz): Symbols are pictures or things that stand for something else. The seal and flag are Maine's symbols.

urban (URR-bun): Urban relates to city life. Many people in Maine live in urban areas.

Further Information

Books

Reynolds, Cynthia Furlong. *L is for Lobster: A Maine Alphabet*. Chelsea, MI: Sleeping Bear Press, 2001.

Webster, Christine. *Maine*. New York: Children's Press, 2008.

Zschock, Martha Day. *Journey around Maine from A to Z*. Beverly, MA: Commonwealth Editions, 2007.

Web Sites

Visit our Web site for links about Maine: *childsworld.com/links*

Note to Parents, Teachers, and Librarians: We routinely verify our Web links to make sure they are safe and active sites. So encourage your readers to check them out!

Index